G000099933

№ CS71.S967 1900

GIVEN BY

William A. Whitcomb

To his cousin and colleague
  William A. Whitcomb
who supplied the most important part
of the recent Addenda, with the
acknowledgements of the author
  Edward Forrester Holden Sutton
      August 20. 1935.

GENEALOGICAL NOTES

OF THE

SUTTON FAMILY

OF NEW JERSEY

BY

EDWARD F. H. SUTTON

[PRINTED FOR PRIVATE CIRCULATION]

NEW YORK
T. A. WRIGHT, Printer and Publisher
1900

PUBLIC LIBRARY
OF THE
CITY OF BOSTON

*C571
.5967
1900

William A Whitcomb
Sept. 26, 1935

PUBLIC LIBRARY
OF THE
CITY OF BOSTON

> *" This firstë stock was full of righteousnesse*
> *True of his word, sober, pitous and free*
> *Clean of his ghost, and lovéd businesse*
> *Against the vice of sloth, in honestee."*
> —Chaucer.

> *" Honour * * * * old virtues, conformable unto*
> *times before you, which are the noblest armoury."*
> —Sir Thomas Browne.

THE FAMILY.

In the New Jersey of a hundred years ago, one family of Suttons was so numerous, that, in the writer's opinion, to bear the name and to derive ancestry from the State is almost proof of membership in it. They were, for the most part, farmers and artisans, attached to the Baptist or Presbyterian creeds, and located chiefly in the northern half of the State—the East Jersey of colonial times. The townships of Piscataway in Middlesex, Tewkesbury in Hunterdon, and especially Bernard in Somerset, with the village of Basking Ridge, may be mentioned as particular family centers. The name is comparatively rare in New Jersey to-day, as the later generations have scattered in all directions. Canada has its representatives, and there is probably not a State in the Union but has been planted with shoots from this old New England stock.

WILLIAM SUTTON.

The first of the family of whom we have record was William Sutton, who appears in Massachusetts in 1666, at Eastham on Cape Cod. As the stream of Puritan immigration had almost dried up twenty years before this date,* it is extremely probable that he represents the second generation in New England. Their proximity suggests a relationship to one or the other of two families of Suttons, respectively, of Hingham † and Scituate, ‡ small towns of old Plymouth Colony directly across the bay from Eastham.

Massachusetts and E.F.H.S.

Careful investigation, however, has failed as yet to establish a connection with either, or to suggest any other line of research. Our history opens, therefore, at Eastham, on the eleventh of July, 1666, with the marriage of William Sutton, yeoman (aged probably twenty-five years), of

---

* See Bancroft's "History of the United States," vol. i., page 468.

† John Sutton, who settled in Hingham, came from Attleborough, in Norfolkshire, arriving in the ship Diligent in 1638, with his wife Julien, a son John, and three other children. He also lived in Rehoboth. He died apparently about 1650; his wife in 1650. From "Vital Records of Rehoboth" the present writer infers that among his children were three, named Esther, Anne, and Margaret.   *1678.*   *1634.*   *1670.*

‡ George Sutton, of Scituate, arrived in 1638. He had a brother Simon, of Scituate, of whom nothing further is known. George married Sarah Tilden, and had children (according to Savage), John, Lydia, Sarah, and Elizabeth.

See Addenda at end of the book for George Sutton's family, and discussion of his relationship to William Sutton.

E.F.H.S.

either English birth or descent, to Damaris, daughter of Alice and Richard Bishop.* Eastham, originally called Nausett, after the name of a local Indian tribe, was at this date a settlement of some twenty years' standing, and numbered some four or five dozen souls—a tiny outpost of English life and civilization, planted upon the "narrow neck of land" between the bleak bay and the bleaker Atlantic. It was in this very year of 1666 that tidings began to spread through New England of the founding of another colony down in the southwest, between the great North† and South Rivers, where settlers were welcome, the Indians friendly, the soil and climate excellent, and civil and religious liberty guaranteed. Many people from all parts of the land of the Puritans migrated to this new country of "the Jerseys;" and about the year 1672 William Sutton also removed, and became a landholder under Berkeley and Carteret. As Cape Cod was one of the few districts in New England where Quakerism gained a footing, and as William

---

* Richard Bishop is noted as a soldier of the colony, in the "Genealogical Register of New England," vol. iv., page 255, second column. When William Sutton removed to New Jersey, Bishop sold his property at Duxbury, Mass., and came to live with him.

† The Hudson and the Delaware.

Sutton in his New Jersey home was an influential Quaker, it is very probable that matters of religious belief had much to do with his departure from Eastham. In the year 1666 a "plantation" of some forty thousand acres was laid out upon the banks of the Raritan, within the bounds of the present Middlesex County, and not far from the spot where a few years later New Brunswick was founded. Its possession was confirmed not only by the white man's title, but by deed from Canackawack and Thingorawis, chiefs of the Naraticong Indians, who were a branch of the Lenni Lenape. As the settlers were mostly from those parts of New Hampshire and Maine which border the Piscataqua River, they called it Piscataqua or Piscataway, in memory of their old home. Here William Sutton pitched his tent, and prospered; for, thanks to fair dealings with the Indians, the wolves and the forest were the only enemies. In 1682, when the town and township numbered some four hundred souls, he was owner of two hundred and forty-nine acres of land, burdened only by the nominal quit-rent of one-half penny per acre annually. Small items of his life, grave or humorous, we glean from the records of more than two centuries ago. A Quaker, he was a pillar of the congregation that

met in the neighboring town of Woodbridge. We
see him a person of some honor in the little com-
munity: chosen freeholder at one time, constable
at another, town-clerk at another, and we find
that, with advancing years, his services were desired upon boards of church discipline and inquiry.
It is recorded that he contributed "a year old
steer" toward the proposed erection of the
Friends' Meeting House at Woodbridge—a dona-
tion that seems to have been a thorn in the flesh
of the finance committee. For two years they
were unable to convert the animal into cash, and
were obliged to board it during three winters at
exorbitant rates, varying from six to eight and
one-half shillings per winter. The growth of
sons to man's estate and matrimony, is marked
in the records by such entries as this:

"William Sutton hath, in consideration of fatherly love and
affection, given and granted to Daniel Sutton, his son, 75 acres
of land."

Finally, in 1713, William is spoken of as an
aged man, and we hear of him no more. Doubtless another year or two brought the end of his
homely and laborious life, and rest in the little
Quaker Churchyard at Woodbridge.

Damaris Bishop, first wife of William Sutton,
died in Piscataway, February 6, 1682-3. He mar-

ried, in that town, Jane Barnes, January 9, 1684–5.

CHILDREN :

1　Alice², b. in Eastham, Mass., May 13, 1668.
2　Thomas², b. in Eastham, Mass., Nov. 11, 1669.
3　Mary², b. in Eastham, Mass., Oct. 4, 1671; m.,
　　Dec. 23, 1689, Daniel McDaniel.
4　John², b. in Piscataway, N. J., April 20, 1674.
5　Judah², b. in Piscataway, N. J., Jan. 24, 1674–5.
6　Richard², b. in Piscataway, N. J., July 18, 1676.
7　Joseph², b. in Piscataway, N. J., June 27, 1678;
　　d. Dec. 19, 1682.
8　Benjamin², b. in Piscataway, N. J., Feb. 24,
　　1679–80; d. Dec. 22, 1682.
9　Daniel², b. in Piscataway, N. J., Feb. 25, 1681–2.
10　Joseph², b. in Piscataway, N. J., Sept. 11, 1693.

THOMAS² (William¹)

Lived at Piscataway.　Married, April, 1693,
Mary Adams of Woodbridge.

CHILDREN :

1　Joseph³, b. about 1694.
2　Rachel³, b. March 27, 1695.
3　Benjamin³, b. Jan. 19, 1696–7.
4　Samuel³, } b. March 16, 1698–9 (twins).
5　Hannah³, }

6 Nathaniel², b. May 23, 1701.
7 Thomas², b. about 1705.

JOHN² (William¹)

Married, about 1695, Elizabeth ———. Removing from Piscataway, he settled at Passaic Valley, in Morris County, N. J., four to five miles from Basking Ridge, in Somerset County. He bought land at Harrison's Neck, N. J., November 11, 1741, and sold Piscataway lands, December 31, 1741. His will (dated December 17, 1746) was probated December 20, 1750; so he must have died that year, aged seventy-six. The will mentions all his children excepting Sarah. His wife Elizabeth died (according to her gravestone in the Baptist Churchyard at Stelton, Piscataway), May 10, 1731, aged fifty-two years.

CHILDREN:

1 Moses³, b. Feb. 2, 1696–7.
2 Aaron³, b. July 2, 1699; married, and died before 1746.
3 John³, b. Sept. 19, 1701.
4 David³, b. July 31, 1703.
5 Sarah³, b. July 21, 1706.
6 James³, b. May 9, 1709.
7 Jesse³, b. July 6, 1711.

8   Mary ³, b. Aug. 15, 1717.
9   Ephraim ³, b. Dec. 7, 1719.

JUDAH ² (William ¹)

Lived at Piscataway.   Married, May 6, 1698, Emma Canter.   (This name may be Carter or Cauter.)

CHILDREN :

1   Emma ³, b. March 9, 1698–9; m. Hugh Dunn, Jr., June 19, 1720.
2   Damaris ³, b. Dec. 18, 1700.
3   Patience ³, b. Jan. 27, 1702–3.
4   William ³, b. Jan. 4, 1706–7.
5   Mary ³, b. July 3, 1709.
6   Sarah ³, b. Feb. 28, 1711.
7   Elizabeth ³, b. Oct. 3, 1713.
8   Anne ³, b. June 25, 1714.
9   Joseph ³, b. Dec. 6, 1716.
10 Rachel ³, b. May 28, 1719.
11 Benjamin ³, b. April 13, 1722.

RICHARD ² (William ¹)

Lived in Piscataway. Married Sarah, daughter of Vincent Rognon (the Huguenot founder of the Runyon family), and Anne Boutcher, an English woman, his wife, January 25, 1702. Richard died in 1732, and his widow in 1736 married James Campbell.

CHILDREN:

1 Sarah³, b. Dec. 31, 1703; m. Joseph Manning.
2 Anna³, b. May 20, 1706; m. Hendrick Sleight.
3 Nathan³, b. Aug. 16, 1708; d. 1733, unmarried.
4 Richard³, b. Feb. 14, 1711–2.
5 Peter³, b. May 2, 1713. (Probably the man
        dying in 1740 at Piscataway. Wife Sarah
        administratrix.)
6 Catherine³, b. Jan. 24, 1715–6.
7 Joshua³, b. Nov. 18, 1718.
8 Jonas³, b. April 18, 1721.
9 Amos³, b. July 16, 1723.
10 Joseph³, b. Aug. 15, 1726.

DANIEL² (William¹)

Married, I., October 31, 1704, Patience, daughter of John and Dorothy Martin, of Piscataway. (John Martin* was one of the four Piscataway grantees. He came from Dover, in the valley of the Piscataqua, in what is now New Hampshire. He was a landholder there in 1648, served on the grand jury in 1654, and was freeman in 1666. His ~~first~~ wife's name was Esther Roberts.) Married, II., August 25, 1724, Lydia Collier, of Woodbridge. In 1719 he was member

Son of John Martin and Esther Roberts. E.F.H.S.

---

* John Martin, Charles Gilman, Hugh Dunn, and Hopewell Hull applied for, and received, December 18, 1666, the Piscataway land grant.

of the board of freeholders. As late as 1729 he is noted as living at Piscataway; but in 1736, when he serves as an executor of his brother Richard's estate, he is said to be a resident of Somerset County. He is probably the man who was dismissed from the Piscataway Baptist Church in 1752, and admitted the same year to the Morristown Baptist Church, where his death is recorded in 1761. His age was seventy-nine years. When we consider the place of residence of his sons, and the fact that he attended church at Morristown, it seems beyond doubt that his Somerset County property was located in Bernard Township, near Basking Ridge, where, as we learn from the Elizabethtown Bill in Chancery, some one of the Suttons had located prior to February, 1729-30. As late as 1735 this part of the county was almost unbroken wilderness.

CHILDREN:

1   Anne², b. Sept. 16, 1705.
2   Zebulon², b. Sept. 1, 1707.
3   Zacharias², b. Oct. 5, 1709.
4   John², b. Aug. 10, 1713.
5   Dorothy², b. May 1, 1717.
6   Patience², b. May 23, 1719; m., about 1752,
          Jonathan⁴ Doty, son of Jonathan³ Doty.
7   Esther², b. Aug. 2, 1721.

8 Daniel³, b. May 8, 1725. (By second wife Lydia Collier.)

JOSEPH ³ (Thomas², William¹)

Of Piscataway. Married, December 25, 1718, Priscilla Langstaff. One tablet stands to the memory of both in St. James' Churchyard, Piscataway, stating that he died March 17, 1762, aged sixty-nine, and she died the same year, aged sixty-three.

CHILDREN :

1 Martha⁴, b. Sept. 3, 1719.
2 Sarah⁴, b. Dec. 1, 1721; d. in infancy.
3 Sarah⁴, b. Feb. 9, 1723.
4 Henry⁴, b. April 6, 1724; d. Oct. 8, 1806, aged eighty-two. (A soldier of the Revolution.*)
5 Joseph⁴, b. Feb. 15, 1728.
6 Jacob⁴, b. July 3, 1730.
7 Priscilla⁴, b. April 14, 1735.

SAMUEL ³ (Thomas², William¹)

Of Piscataway. Married, about 1725, Martha ———.

---

* For an inventory of his losses during the war, see page 25.

CHILDREN (LIST PROBABLY INCOMPLETE):

1 Sarah⁴, b. March 12, 1726.
2 Amaziah⁴, b. Jan. 4, 1728–9.
3 Hannah⁴, b. Dec. 4, 1730.

THOMAS³ (Thomas², William¹)

Of Piscataway. Married, January 6, 1734–5, Mary Lewis.

CHILDREN (LIST INCOMPLETE):

1 Nehemiah⁴, b. Sept. 28, 1735.

MOSES³ (John², William¹)

Married, about 1717, Yanick ———. (The name is so written in the record; it probably stands for the Dutch "Jannetje.") He removed from Piscataway to Bedminster Township, Somerset County, about 1737, in which year he is recorded as living in Lamington and selling land at Piscataway. He seems also to have lived at Peapack, in Bedminster Township. His eldest son, John, was appointed administrator of his estate in 1740; so he doubtless died in that year, aged forty-three.

CHILDREN (BORN IN PISCATAWAY):

1 John⁴, b. June 18, 1718.
2 Aaron⁴, b. March 17, 1718–9.
3 Martha⁴, b. Feb. 15, 1722.
4 Susanna⁴, b. May 14, 1723.
5 Hugh⁴, b. about 1725. ⎱ *
6 Levi⁴, b. about 1727. ⎰

JOHN³ (John², William¹)

Resided in Somerset County. Married Mary ———, and probably died in 1761, aged sixty, as in that year his will was probated. The will is authority for the names of his children.

CHILDREN:

1 Elizabeth⁴.
2 Anna⁴.
3 Lois⁴, b. ———; m. Thomas, son of Richard Smith.
4 Mary⁴, b. ———; m. Elijah, son of Richard Smith. (She was not of age in 1758, the date of the will.)
5 Jeremiah⁴.
6 Abner⁴, b. ———; ~~deceased at the date of the will, 1758.~~
7 Philip⁴.

---

* These two Bedminster Township Suttons are assigned to Moses' family on grounds of probability.

He was not "deceased at the date of the will," which I have since seen. This is the Rev. Abner of p. 47. b. May 8. 1741. E.F.H.S.

DAVID³ (John², William¹)

Of Basking Ridge, Bernard Township, Somerset County. Died between December 1 and December 19, 1775, the respective dates of the drawing and probating of his will. He was then aged seventy-two years. The will mentions his wife (without giving her name) and names his children.

CHILDREN (NOT KNOWN TO BE IN ORDER OF BIRTH):

1   Isaac⁴, b. ———. (Noted as the eldest; m. Rachel Doty.)
2   David⁴.
3   John⁴, b. 1733; m. Ruth Stout; d. about 1813, aged eighty.
4   Abraham⁴.
5   James⁴.
6   Moses⁴.
7   Sarah⁴.
8   Elizabeth⁴, b. ———. (Her three youngest daughters were named Marah, Joanna, and Abigail.)
9   Mary⁴, b. ———; d. 1746. (Had a son David.)

The four brothers—Isaac⁴, David⁴, John⁴, and James⁴—were all Baptist clergymen and missionaries to Tennessee. Isaac⁴ is the ancestor of the Suttons of Fayette County, Pa. James⁴ settled in Kentucky. John⁴ also settled in Kentucky, at

Rev. John Sutton and Rev. John Manning were the Commissioners of the New Jersey Baptists who obtained from Rhode Island the charter of Brown University. Manning, its first President, had a Fitzrandolph for a mother, near cousin of Nathaniel Fitzrandolph, who gave the land for the founding of Princeton University. E.F.H.S.

Harrodsburgh, and left a numerous posterity. As an early advocate of emancipation, and as a successful worker in a large and difficult field, he has earned for himself an honorable place in the history of his adopted State. He was educated at Hopewell, N. J., ordained at Scotch Plains in 1763, and began his work as a missionary to Nova Scotia. Previous to his final removal to Kentucky, he had charges at Newport, R. I., Salem and Cape May, N. J., and Welsh Tract, Del.; and at other times he labored in Pennsylvania, Virginia, and Tennessee.

EPHRAIM² (John², William¹)

Of Passaic Valley. Lived on "Sutton's Hill." He doubtless died in 1790, aged seventy-one, for in that year his will was probated. It mentions his wife Phœbe and four children.

CHILDREN :

1 James⁴ Governeur.
2 David⁴.
3 Jesse⁴.
4 William⁴, b. ——; m. Lavina, "a Dutch girl." (After William's death the family removed to Ohio. The date of removal is perhaps indicated by the fact that Lavina and her children — then living in Bernardsville, Somerset County—sold land in 1801.)

ZEBULON³ (Daniel², William¹)

Of Bernard Township, Somerset County, on February 28, 1746-7, leased of James Alexander [fa]ther of William Alexander, the Lord Stirling [of R]evolutionary fame) one hundred and thirty [acre]s of land, bordering on the Passaic River and [nex]t to John Doty.* The Dotys are an old New [Je]rsey family, and have been associated with [an]d have intermarried with the Suttons from the [ea]rliest times. They are descended of Samuel [D]oty (a son of Edward, the Mayflower Pilgrim), [w]ho removed from Eastham, on Cape Cod, and [se]ttled at Piscataway. So many Dotys went to [t]he neighborhood of Basking Ridge, that (to use [t]he words of the author of the "Doty Genealogy") [t]he town was like a Doty settlement." All of [Z]ebulon Sutton's brothers acquired land, either [b]y lease or purchase, of the Alexander estate, a [t]ract of some 800 acres, which was a portion of [t]he original "Harrison's Purchase," and included the town of Basking Ridge. Zachariah Sutton †

---

* John Doty leased 300 acres of the Alexander estate in 1739. The Alexander property consisting only of some 800 acres, John and Jonathan Doty and the four Sutton brothers must have occupied most of it. John Doty, 300 acres; Zeb. Sutton, 130 acres; Zach. Sutton, 100 acres; John Sutton, 85 acres. Total, 615 acres.

† One of the three brothers of Zebulon Sutton had a son, Zebulon, who served in the Revolution, afterward removed to Knox County, Ohio, and died there at a good old age. His pension papers are on file at Washington.

eased, April 26, 1746, 100 acres. Daniel leased a
tract, April 7, 1749, and John, on August 13, 1749,
bought for £96 17 s., Jersey money, 84 87/100
acres of land. The town of Basking Ridge dates
from about 1720, and is situated, as its name
implies, upon a sharply rising ground. It lies in
the finest agricultural region of the State, one of
low rolling hills, which Stirling found a suitable
environment for his famous manor, where were
entertained so many of the notables of the Revolution. This disappeared a century or more ago;
but the region has again, in these modern days,
become noted for its beautiful country-seats.
About and in the old town marched and encamped
the French and Continental armies, and in its
tavern the traitor Lee was captured by English
troopers, and removed from further interference
with the fortunes of the American cause. Zebulon Sutton, according to his son Uriah, lived at
the town of North Branch. He attended the old
Presbyterian Church at Basking Ridge. He married, about 1731, Mary ———, probably in Piscataway. Her surname was probably Doty,*

?? E.F.H.S.

---

* Family names, neighborhood, and association, and the intimacy
shown by intermarriage (Patience[3] Sutton and Jonathan[4] Doty) make it
seem probable that Zebulon Sutton's wife's name was Mary Doty. This
could not be the case if the date of Jonathan[3] Doty's marriage was 1717, as
the author of the "Doty Genealogy" *estimates*. There is nothing to show
that the marriage did not take place earlier.

aughter (born about 1713) of Jonathan[3] Doty,
of Piscataway, and Mary, his wife. Jonathan[3]
Doty* removed to Basking Ridge and leased a
'arm from the Alexander estate (close to the one
soon after occupied by Zebulon Sutton) in 1739.
He was a son of Samuel Doty and Jane Harman,
and a grandson of Edward Doty (the Mayflower
Pilgrim) and Faith Clarke.

CHILDREN :†

1 Patience[4], b. May 31, 1732.
2 Jonathan[4], b. March 23, 1735.
3 Jeremiah[4], b. Oct. 29, 1738.
4 Uriah[4], b. July 21, 1741.
5 Peter[4], b. about 1743.
6 Mary[4], b. Sept. 19, 1744.
7 Joseph[4], b. July 9, 1747.
8 Anna[4], b. Dec. 30, 1750.

---

* Jonathan[3] Doty was born 1687-8, and married to Mary about 1712
(author of "Doty Genealogy" *estimates* 1717); Samuel[2] Doty was born 1643,
died 1715, married, November 15, 1678, Jane Harman of Piscataway. Edward[1]
Doty came on the Mayflower, 1620, died August 23, 1655, married, January 6,
1634-5, Faith (born 1619), daughter of Faith and Thurston Clarke. Thurston
Clarke came to Plymouth in 1634, having sailed April 30th of that year from
Ipswich in Suffolkshire on the ship Francis.

† The Bible which contained the original of Zebulon[3] Sutton's family
record has long been lost. A transcript of the latter was made by his grandson, Shadrach[5] Sutton (son of Joseph[4]) some seventy or eighty years ago.
This is now in possession of Shadrach's niece, Mrs. Nancy C. Sutton Axtell,
of Minneapolis, Minn., and is the present writer's authority. It does not
contain the name of Peter[4]. Reasons for adding Peter's name will be
discussed in connection with his family.

ONATHAN [4] (Zebulon [3], Daniel [2], William [1])

Lived in Bedminster Township, Somerset ounty, where he paid, in 1787, taxes on one hunred and fifty acres of land, amounting to £2, 12 s., d. He married, about 1761, Rachel Colyer, who as born March 12, 1740. He was a member of he Presbyterian Church at Basking Ridge, and fter his removal, about 1789-90, to Sparta, in ussex County, was an elder in the local Presbyerian Church until his death, on February 2, 818, at the age of eighty-three years. His wife, Rachel, died at Sparta, April 12, 1810, aged eventy years.

Jonathan [4] was a Revolutionary soldier,* and, like his brother Uriah, held a captain's commission. He was always referred to by his immediate descendants as "the captain." The facts of his service and losses, the hardships and suffering of his wife and children during his absence in the field, owing to the ravages of the Hessians, we have from the statements of his son Jacob lied 1852) and Jacob's wife, Hannah (died 1862), o their grandson, the Rev. J. Ford Sutton, D.D.

* Unfortunately, Jonathan [4] Sutton's name does not appear in the "Official Register of the Officers and Men of New Jersey" (compiled by Adjutant-General Stryker). The author, however, does not claim that the "Register" is absolutely complete, since the rolls from which it was compiled were often very carelessly kept and quite imperfect.

Jonathan Sutton's Record Discovered. He was Sergeant in Capt. John Polhemus' company, 1st Regt. New Jersey troops from Oct 29th 1775. (Signed) the Military Sec. War Department Washington D.C. J. F. S.

(born 1827). From this authority we learn that Jonathan[4], and his brothers Uriah[4] and Joseph[4], were present at the battle of Monmouth, and bore their testimony to the great suffering of the troops on account of the intense heat. We are told how his family would sit up all night to make cartridges, with windows darkened for fear of spies, and how the Hessians came and pitched the sheaves from the stacks of wheat till their horses waded "up to the belly" in it, and how, turning the mother and children out of the house, they plundered it of what they desired, and destroyed the remainder. How near Captain Jonathan came to losing the powder that was in his charge is another incident. He had removed it from its hiding-place under a stack of buckwheat straw only the night before a squad of cavalry came in search of it. They tore the stack to pieces, and were much exasperated to find only the place where it had lain.

CHILDREN :

1 Zebulon[5], b. Feb. 1, 1762.
2 Mary[5], b. ———; never married.
3 Sarah[5], b. ———; never married.
4 Hannah[5], b. ———; m. Jos. Miller. (No issue.)
5 Rebecca[5], b. ———; m. Cornelius Wiesner.
6 Jacob[5], b. Oct. 12, 1773.

The following account of the losses in the Revolution of Henry[4] Sutton (Joseph[3], Thomas[2], William[1]) may be of interest. Henry[4] was a private of N. J. State Troops, and one of the Middlesex County "Committee of Observation:"

*" Inventory of Sundries taken and destroyed by the Enemy and their Adherents, the property of Henry Sutton, of Piscataway, Middlesex County :

		£ S.D.
1776. Dec[r]. & in 1777.	"To 6554 Rails in fence, midling good	49. 0.0
	2100 Stakes " " "	7.17.6
	5 Tons of fresh Hay	12.10.0
	6 do. of Salt Hay @ home	9. 0.0
	3 do. of do. in the Meadows	3. 0.0
	40 Bushels Wheat & 20 do. of Rye in Sheaf	13.15.0
	1 Yoke of Oxen, midling large	15. 0.0
	1 Year old Bull 25/. 20 Sheep £10.	11. 5.0
	50 lb. Flax in the rough	18.9
	9 acres of Wheat in the Ground	13.10.0
	Timber cut & destroyed to the amount of	7. 0.0
	2770 Rails & 900 Stakes at the place that was Capt. Langstaff's	23. 0.0
	1 Barn Burnt on place £30. House on do. place destroyed by 3 floors taken out, the Boards taken off, the chimney & walls down, £25.	55. 0.0
	20 Fruit Trees	3. 0.0
		£223.16.3

"Henry Sutton being sworn saith that the above Inventory is just and true. And that he was knowing to Sundry of the

---

* From Original MSS., Vol. No. 172. State Library at Trenton, N. J.

said Articles being taken by the British Troops, and that he had Sufficient reason to believe the said Troops took all the remainder of the said Articles. And that he had not received any satisfaction for any one thing therein contained.

"Sworn before me Jos. Olden }   Henry Sutton.

"Thomas Holtom being Sworn Saith that he was called to View the damages done to the building that Henry Sutton purchas'd of Capt. Henry Langstaff, being done by the British Troops, &, having considered of the same, do adjudge the said damages to the amount of £55. o.o.

"Sworn before me Jos. Olden }   Thomas Holtom."

ZEBULON⁵ (Jonathan⁴, Zebulon³, Daniel², William¹)

Married, March 2, 1786, Mary, born August 30, 1768, daughter of Edward and Martha Lewis. He died July 1, 1826, at Newfoundland, N. J., and was buried there. His wife, Mary, removed to Pennsylvania, and died April 7, 1856. He was an elder of the Presbyterian Church, and a soldier of the Revolution (see Stryker's "Officers and Men of New Jersey," page 776). His descendants, by the line of his eldest son Nathan, live at Gardner, Grundy County, Ill.

CHILDREN :

1   Martha⁶, b. June 22, 1787; m. Henry Brasted.
2   Nathan⁶, b. April 12, 1789; m. Martha Beardsley, and died in Illinois, March 30, 1879.

3 Lewis⁶, b. July 12, 1791; m. Jane Ketcham,
      and died 1867.
4 Mark⁶, b. Aug. 17, 1802.

MARK⁶ (Zebulon⁵, Jonathan⁴, Zebulon³, Daniel²,
    William¹)

Married, December 6, 1826, Lydia Young,
born August 4, 1803. His descendants live at
Muncy, Lycoming County, Pa.

CHILDREN:

1 Zebulon⁷ B., b. Oct. 4, 1827; d. Dec. 12, 1890.
2 Mary⁷ E., b. Jan. 30, 1830; m., Oct. 5, 1858,
      Samuel Sprout.
3 Sarah⁷ M., b. May 5, 1832; m., April 20, 1856,
      Stephen F. Edsell.
4 Martha⁷ L., b. Feb. 22, 1835.
5 Susan⁷ A., b. May 18, 1837; d. July 15, 1837.
6 Lavinia⁷ G., b. Aug. 2, 1839; m., May 7, 1864,
      Allan Welch, and d. Dec. 26, 1890.
7 James⁷ E., b. April 8, 1843; d. March 26, 1853.

JACOB⁵ (Jonathan⁴, Zebulon³, Daniel², William¹)

Lived in Hardyston Township, Sussex County,
N. J. Married, March 18, 1797, Hannah Rorick
—born April 21, 1777. (She was daughter of
Michael Rorick, born in Bergen County, April 10,
1749, died at Franklin Furnace, Sussex County,

October 28, 1832; and Lucretia Hardin, born in Massachusetts, February 21, 1752, died at Franklin Furnace, September 12, 1834: they were married in 1774. The name Rorick was originally spelled Röhrig, and is probably of Palatine German origin.) Jacob Sutton died December 27, 1852, aged seventy-nine; his wife died March 27, 1862, aged eighty-five.

CHILDREN :

1 Michael⁶ Rorick, b. Nov. 16, 1797.
2 Rebecca⁶, b. Dec. 7, 1799; m. Samuel Bedell.
3 Lewis⁶, b. Jan. 6, 1802.
4 Jacob⁶, b. Nov. 5, 1804.
5 Jonathan⁶, b. Dec. 24, 1807.
6 John⁶ Rorick, b. Nov. 13, 1810.
7 Catharine⁶,* b. Aug. 9, 1813; m. Wm. Van Blarcom.
8 William⁶ Inglis, b. June 23, 1817.

MICHAEL⁶ RORICK (Jacob⁵, Jonathan⁴, Zebulon³, Daniel², William¹)

Lived in Hardyston Township, Sussex County, N. J., near Franklin Furnace. Married, March 29, 1822, Elizabeth Forrester, born January 23,

---

* She died April 19, 1891, survived by six children. One of these, Captain Lewis Van Blarcom, is a leading lawyer of Sussex County. He married, August 17, 1871, Mary, daughter of Dr. Alexander H. Thompson, and has children, Katharine and Andrew.

1799. She was daughter of Peter Forrester (son of an Englishman, John Forrester, and Anna ~~Van Buskirk, a woman of Dutch descent~~) and Katharine Pietersen (daughter of Daniel Pietersen, a man of Dutch ancestry, and Eva Hardt*). Michael R. Sutton died January 6, 1881, aged eighty-four, in Romeo, Mich., whither he removed in 1856. His wife died in Romeo, January 6, 1865, aged sixty-six.

BRISCARRICK
Highland Scotch.
E.F.H.S.

CHILDREN :

1 Hannah', b. Aug. 12, 1823; m. Joseph Ayres.
2 Lucy', b. Jan. 7, 1825; m. Manuel Sibbet.
3 Joseph Ford', b. July 15, 1827.
4 Katharine', b. May 30, 1829; d. 1884, unmarried.
5 Elias Fairchild', b. June 25, 1831.
7 Matilda Fairchild', b. Dec. 30, 1834; m. Wm. L. Barclay.
6 Amos Munson', b. Jan. 15, 1835; m. Joanna Bates; d. March 24, 1884.

---

* The father of Eva Hardt, who married Daniel Pietersen, was a well-to-do German of the Rhenish Palatinate. He fled from the civil and religious disturbances of his native state to America about 1735, accompanied by his wife, his daughter Eva, and four other children. He had paid passage for all in full; but, when he died at sea, the captain of the vessel not only seized the entire effects of the widow (including some valuable old silver), but, on reaching port, sold her and her children as redemptioners. Such abuses were only too common in those days. A reminiscence of Eva Hardt's old home on the Rhine is perhaps not unworthy of notice, as showing how slight a tradition may survive the lapse of nearly two centuries. Her father owned a vineyard, and in the time of the vintage she and other children, standing at upper windows of opposite houses, would fill their mouths with the sweet must, and try which could spurt it farthest into the street below. It may be imagined that, in thrifty German households, this did not occur very often.

JOSEPH [7] **FORD** (Michael [6], Jacob [5], Jonathan [4], Zebulon [3], Daniel [2], William [1])

Resides in New York City. A. B., Rutgers College, 1852, A. M., 1855; Union Theological Seminary, 1857, and ordained minister of the Presbyterian Church the same year; D. D., Marysville College, 1883; chaplain 102d Regiment New York Volunteer Infantry, 1862; general agent United States Christian Commission, Department of the Gulf, 1863. Fellow of the American Geographical Society. Married, I., Eliza Storrs, April 12, 1859, daughter of Horace Holden, Esq., of New York City, and Mary Cotton. She was born December 23, 1829; died August 6, 1860. Married, II., Katharine Judson Holden, daughter of Horace Holden, Esq., and Katharine Plant Judson, April 10, 1866. She was born April 26, 1838; died December 30, 1898.

CHILDREN :

1 Horace [8] Holden, b. July 6, 1867 ; d. Nov. 13, 1874.
2 Joseph [8] Holden, b. Oct. 23, 1869. (A. B., Princeton, 1890, A. M., 1893; LL. B., New York Law School, 1893.)
3 Daniel [8] Judson, b. May 17, 1872 ; d. Nov. 30, 1874.

d. 1902.

E.F.H.S.

4   Edward[6] Forrester Holden, b. Feb. 15, 1874.
        (A. B., Princeton, 1895; M. D., Columbia,
        1899.)
5   Frederick[6] Judson Holden, b. June 3, 1876.
        (A. B., Princeton, 1898.)

ELIAS[7] FAIRCHILD (Michael[6], Jacob[5], Jona-
    than[4], Zebulon[3], Daniel[2], William[1])

Resides at Lake Linden, Mich.   Married, September 5, 1865, Mary, b. June 7, 1843, daughter
of William Harris and Elizabeth Tregoning, of
Lake Linden.

CHILDREN :

1   Elizabeth[8], b. June 24, 1868.
2   Walter[8] Harris, b. June 18, 1885.

JONATHAN[6] (Jacob[5], Jonathan[4], Zebulon[3], Dan-
    iel[2], William[1])

Removed to Oakland County, Mich., and there
died, December 5, 1874.   Married Delilah Pred-
more, born in Sussex County, N. J., February 21,
1815, and died at Romeo, Mich., April 3, 1893.

CHILDREN :

1   Joshua[7] P., b. June 27, 1837.
2   Jemima[7] R., b. Dec. 13, 1840; m., 1856, Joel W.
        Linderman.

3 Amzy ⁷ R., b. April 23, 1842.
4 Joseph ⁷ D., b. April 26, 1845.
5 Hannah ⁷ M., b. March 20, 1846; d. Sept. 18, 1864.
6 Adelia ⁷ C., b. Jan. 22, 1849; d. Sept. 3, 1865.
7 Edward ⁷ M., b. May 30, 1850; d. Jan. 1, 1893.
8 Drusilla ⁷ D., b. Aug. 8, 1851; m., 1867, Daniel
       W. Bennett.
9 Elmer ⁷ B., b. March 20, 1853.

JOSHUA⁷ PREDMORE (Jonathan⁶, Jacob⁵, Jonathan⁴, Zebulon³, Daniel², William¹)

Married, April 25, 1863, Mary E. Shadbolt, of Orion, Mich.; she was born April 10, 1840. He resides at Kansas City, Mo.

CHILDREN :

1 Linton⁸ Beach, b. Sept. 17, 1865.
2 Archie⁸ L., b. Feb. 15, 1868; d. Jan. 6, 1871.
3 Bessie⁸, b. Nov. 13, 1869; m., Oct. 12, 1893,
       Luther C. Slavens, Jr., of Kansas City.

JOSEPH⁷ DUNLAP (Jonathan⁶, Jacob⁵, Jonathan⁴, Zebulon³, Daniel², William¹)

Resides in Kansas City. Married, April 3, 1883, Eliza Gist Ferguson, born at St. Louis, June 15, 1861.

CHILDREN :

1 Edwin⁸ Arnold, b. Jan. 18, 1884.
2 Josephine⁸, b. June 15, 1890.

AMZY[7] R. (Jonathan[6], Jacob[5], Jonathan[4], Zebulon[3], Daniel[2], William[1])

Married, in 1864, Sarah A. Coates, of Oakville, Ontario.

CHILDREN :

1 Gertrude[8] E., b. March 20, 1865.
2 Marvil[8] C., b. June 23, 1867.

ELMER[7] BEACH (Jonathan[6], Jacob[5], Jonathan[4], Zebulon[3], Daniel[2], William[1])

A prominent lawyer of Sault Ste. Marie, Mich. Married Anna A. Scranton, of Sault Ste. Marie, born December 24, 1863.

LEWIS[6] (Jacob[5], Jonathan[4], Zebulon,[3] Daniel[2], William[1])

Married, November 8, 1823, Elizabeth Losey, born March 12, 1804. He removed to Clarkston, Mich., and there died, July 27, 1852. His wife died August 5, 1898.

CHILDREN :

1 Harriet[7] F., b. Oct. 6, 1824; m. Samuel Groover, March 22, 1842.
2 Cornelius[7] L., b. Dec. 26, 1827 ; m. Elizabeth Brower, June 11, 1850.
3 Abigail[7] M., b. July 22, 1829 ; m. Ebenezer T. Beardslee, May 15, 1851.

4 Susan⁷ T., b. May 2, 1836; m. Charles Beardslee,
       June 11, 1856.
5 Marion⁷ L., b. Dec. 24, 1838; m. Ada Palmer.
6 Delphina⁷ M., b. Feb. 11, 1845; m. Isaac H.
       Lawrence, Jan. 1, 1866.

JACOB⁶ (Jacob⁵, Jonathan⁴, Zebulon³, Daniel²,
   William¹)

Married, December 4, 1825, Teresa Cox, who
was born January 3, 1810, and died May 22, 1891.
He died March 26, 1891. He resided in Sussex
County, N. J.

CHILDREN :

1   Reuben⁷ R., b. Oct. 7, 1826; d. July 2, 1894;
       m. Elizabeth Fox.
2   Martin⁷ C., b. July 7, 1829; m. Mary Bray.
3   Esther⁷ C., b. Dec. 23, 1832; d. Aug. 20, 1860;
       m. Henry Fox.
4   Lemuel⁷ F., b. April 30, 1833; d. Feb. 19, 1897;
       m. Eleanor Westfall.
5   Emily⁷, b. Aug. 26, 1835; d. June 12, 1870.
6   John⁷ H., b. Oct. 23, 1838; m., Jan. 2, 1872, Mary
       Benjamin.
7   George⁷ M., b. Oct. 24, 1840; m. Harriet Mack-
       erley.
8   Dayton⁷ C., b. Jan. 10, 1843; m. Abigail Farber.
9   Teresa⁷ M., b. March 24, 1845; m. Rev. A. J.
       Adams.
10 Georgiana⁷ L., b. Aug. 12, 1857; m. John C.
       Tibbits.

JOHN [6] **RORICK** (Jacob [5], Jonathan [4], Zebulon [3], Daniel [2], William [1])

Married, in 1836, Jemima Stoll. He removed to Racine, Wis., and died there, November 24, 1848.

CHILDREN :

1 Lewis [7] H., b. Aug. 28, 1837.
2 Delphina [7], b. Dec. 28, 1839.
3 George [7] B., b. Feb. 24, 1842.
4 John [7] R., b. Feb. 5, 1844.
5 Theodore [7] D., b. March 24, 1846.
6 Estella [7], b. Aug. 19, 1847.

WILLIAM [6] **INGLIS** (Jacob [5], Jonathan [4], Zebulon [3], Daniel [2], William [1])

Married, February 4, 1840, Mary Stoll. He removed to Clarkston, Mich., and died there, March 11, 1897. His wife died November 22, 1864.

CHILDREN :

1 Jacob [7] R.
2 Abram [7].
3 William [7] H.
4 Anna [7] M.
5 George [7] Edward.
6 Franklin [7] Pierce.
7 Amos [7] H.
8 Sarah [7] E.
9 Joseph [7] F.

URIAH[4] (Zebulon[3], Daniel[2], William[1])

Lived at Kimballs Mountain, in Somerset County, N. J., and attended the Presbyterian Church at Basking Ridge.* He was a captain of New Jersey State Troops (see Stryker's "Officers and Men of New Jersey," page 413), and there is record of his presence at the battles of Monmouth, Watsessing, and Connecticut Farms. His granddaughter, Mrs. Ruth Howell, states that, when the Continental Army lay at Morristown, Washington often dined at his house. A large dog used to follow the general about, and on its back Uriah's little son Stephen (Mrs. Howell's father) was often allowed to ride. Uriah Sutton married, about 1772, Elizabeth Bockover, born November 26, 1751, and died November 13, 1815. Uriah attained the great age of ninety-eight years, dying in 1839, at the home of his son Stephen in Bound Brook, N. J. He was blind for nearly thirty years before his death.

CHILDREN (ORDER OF BIRTH UNKNOWN):

1 Stephen[5], b. Feb. 2, 1775.

---

* Prior to 1800 the following Suttons are recorded as pew-holders in the trustee-book of the Basking Ridge Presbyterian Church (records antedating 1770, it should be said, were destroyed by fire): Zachariah, pew 20; year, 1770. Jeremiah, pew 70; year, 1770. Peter, pew 71; year, 1770. Uriah, pew 72; year, 1770. Jonathan, pew 55; year, 1770. Zebulon, pew 72; year 1783. John, pew 40; year, 1795.

2 Peter[5], b. ——— (named for his paternal
    uncle); d. unmarried.

3 Polly[5], b. ———; m. Johnson.

4 Phœbe[5], b. ——— [probably named for her
    (paternal) uncle Peter's wife]; m. Norris.

5 Ann[5], b. Aug. 9, 1778; m. Barnabas Doty.

6 Katharine[5].

7 Gertrude[5], b. ———; m. Brush.

STEPHEN[5] (Uriah[4], Zebulon[3], Daniel[2], William[1])

Lived first at Liberty Corner, Bernard Township, Somerset County, N. J., afterwards at Bound Brook, and died March 9, 1846. Married, I., about 1798, Sarah Bedell, born March 31, 1781; d. January 21, 1807. Married, II., about 1808, Abigail Martin, born May 31, 1786 (born Compton).

CHILDREN:

1 Katharine[6], b. July 30, 1800; d. Oct. 15, 1822;
    m. Abner P. Howell.

2 Letitia[6], b. Aug. 31, 1801.

3 Ruth[6], b. Oct. 29, 1802; m., I., Elbert Baldwin
    of Newark; m., II., Abner P. Howell, of
    Newark. (She was living in 1895.)

4 Eliza[6], b. Feb. 4, 1804.

5 Uriah[6], b. Jan. 12, 1806.

By the second wife, the following, all of whom removed to the vicinity of Springfield, Ill.:

6 Sarah[6], b. Jan. 10, 1809.

7 Abner [6] M., b. March 19, 1810; d. at Spring-
      field, Ill.

8 Abigail [6], b. Feb. 15, 1812.

9 Stephen [6], b. Jan. 17, 1815; d. at Jacksonville, Ill.

10 Gawin [6] A., b. April 8, 1816. (Note that this
      name occurs in the family of Peter [4]
      Sutton, brother of Uriah [4].)

11 Phœbe [6], b. May 20, 1818.

12 Caroline [6], b. Nov. 17, 1819; d. in infancy.

13 Joseph [6], b. Feb. 22, 1823.

14 Caroline [6], b. July 13, 1826.

15 Mary [6] Louisa, b. Nov. 13, 1828; m. Dr. Sturges,
      of Macon, Ill., where she lives.

PETER [4]* (Zebulon [3], Daniel [2], William [1])

Lived at Basking Ridge, and attended the

---

* The following are the reasons for adding Peter[4] Sutton's name to the family record of Zebulon[3] Sutton (Daniel[2], William[1]). (*Vide supra:*)

I. Statement by Uriah[4] Sutton's grandson, Daniel Doty, who was living, at the age of nearly ninety years, at Liberty Corner, N. J., in 1897, and who knew his grandfather well for thirty years before his death; that Uriah[4] had a favorite brother Peter, of whom he often spoke, and for whom he (Uriah) named his second son.

II. Statement by aged descendants of Peter Sutton in Indiana County, Pa.: that he had a great fondness for the name Uriah, and that he treated the grandchild to whom he gave this name with particular affection.

III. Statement of an aged descendant of Peter Sutton in Indiana County, Pa.: that Mary, Peter's daughter, named a son Jonathan for her father's brother.

IV. The facts that similar accounts of Peter Sutton's escape from the Indians were current among both Peter's descendants in Indiana County, Pa., and Uriah's in New Jersey, though the two families had been separated for a hundred years, and had no knowledge of their kinship.

V. From the occurrence of the unusual name Gawin among both Uriah's and Peter's descendants.

VI. Jonathan and Peter Sutton both enlisted the 1st Regt. New Jersey Troops for the same term service, the one on Oct. 29th 1775 as Sergeant, the one on the following day Oct. 30th 1775 as Private. Address The Military [illegible] War Department Washington D.C.

J. F. S.

Presbyterian Church there. He was a soldier of the Revolution (see Stryker's "Officers and Men of New Jersey," page 776). He married, about 1768, Phœbe Kinnan. In 1796 he removed from Basking Ridge, and in June of that year bought a farm in that part of Westmoreland County, Pa., which is now Indiana County. Subsequently he sold the farm and established an inn on the road from Kitanning, east (which was afterwards the Philadelphia turnpike), and on the spot where the town of Indiana now stands. Among his descendants are numbered some of the most influential residents of the county, in times past and present. His will was probated April 29–30, 1829; so he doubtless died that year, aged about eighty-six. A tradition, current among Suttons both in Indiana County and in New Jersey, states that Peter Sutton was, in his younger days, captured by a band of Indians, to whom he had made himself obnoxious. At nightfall a huge fire was lighted, and a council assembled about it, to determine what should be done with him. Supposing that he did not understand their language, they discussed freely the tortures to be inflicted. Some suggested flaying alive, others burning at the stake, and so on. They had not taken the precaution to bind their captive, and he, at an

opportune moment, seized a young Indian who chanced to be near, pitched him into the fire, and ran for his life. The diversion thus created gave him a little start, and reaching a stream which was crossed by means of a big log, he plunged in and hid himself under it. When his pursuers had passed over it, he made good his escape.

CHILDREN :

1   Gawin[5], b. ———. (Note that this name occurs among the children of Stephen, son of Uriah[4], Peter's[4] brother.)

2   Malachia[5].

3   Mary[5], b. ———; m. Sylvanus Ayres.

4   Thomas[5], b. March 5, 1784.

5   Phœbe[5].

6   Peter[5], b. ———. (Had a son *Uriah*, who died in infancy.)

THOMAS[5] (Peter[4], Zebulon[3], Daniel[2], William[1])

Lived at Indiana, Pa. Married, April 1, 1809, Rebecca Loughrey, born December 8, 1787. He died in 1833, aged forty-nine.

CHILDREN :

1   Rebecca[6], b. Jan. 8, 1810.

2   Phœbe[6], b. April 7, 1811.

3   James[6], b. April 23, 1812.

4 John⁶, b. May 20, 1814; m., in 1847, Mary A.
    Walker; d. June 9, 1877.
5 Thomas⁶, b. Dec. 31, 1815.
6 Mary⁶, b. Oct. 29, 1817.
7 William⁶, b. Aug. 2, 1819.
8 Peter⁶, b. July 24, 1822.
9 Margaret⁶, b. Aug. 21, 1825.
10 Robert⁶, b. April 10, 1828. (A Presbyterian
    clergyman of Cincinnati.)
11 David⁶, b. ———, 1830; d. in infancy.

JAMES⁶ (Thomas⁵, Peter⁴, Zebulon³, Daniel²,
    William¹)

Married, September 3, 1840, Sarah Stansbury,*
born May 27, 1816; died March, 1899. He died
September 10, 1870. He resided at Indiana, Pa.

CHILDREN:

1 Rhodes⁷ Stansbury, b. July 8, 1841.
2 Elizabeth⁷, b. Sept. 19, 1843.
3 Thomas⁷, b. Oct. 14, 1845; m. Mary L. Ander-
    son. (Lives in Russell, Kan.)
4 Clara⁷ R., b. April 6, 1847.
5 William⁷ B., b. Feb. 12, 1849; m. Agnes Black,
    1869. (Lives in Russell, Kan.)
6 James⁷, b. Sept. 9, 1851; d. July 1, 1852.
7 John⁷ A., b. June 6, 1853.

---

* Her grandfather was the first surveyor-general of the State of
Delaware, and for some time was partner in business with Robert Morris,
of Revolutionary fame.

8   Rebecca[7], b. July 20, 1855; d. March 8, 1856.
9   Arthur[7] D., b. Dec. 4, 1857; m. Katharine
        Johnston. (Lives in Beaver Co., Pa.)
10 Helen[7] S., b. July 14, 1860; m. Wm. J. Moore,
        M. D., of Westfield, N. Y.

RHODES[7] STANSBURY (James[6], Thomas[5], Peter[4], Zebulon[3], Daniel[2], William[1])

A leading surgeon of Pittsburgh, Pa. A. B., Washington and Jefferson College, 1862; A. M., 1865; attached to Medical Department of Union Army, 1863–4; M. D., University of Pennsylvania, 1865; LL. D., Wooster University, 1886; gynæcologist to the Allegheny General Hospital at Pittsburgh, and surgeon of the Terrace Bank Sanatorium of Allegheny. He married, April 17, 1867, Josephine, daughter of the Hon. James McCullough, of Canonsburgh, Pa.

CHILDREN :

1   Stansbury[8], b. Nov. 15, 1869.
2   Eliza[8] McCullough, b. June 23, 1871; m. A.
        Hartupee McKee, of Pittsburgh.

JOHN[7] A. (James[6], Thomas[5], Peter[4], Zebulon[3], Daniel[2], William[1])

Married, September 9, 1875, Anne Gilchrist

Woods, who was born in Allegheny County, Pa., June 27, 1853.   He resides in Pittsburgh, Pa.

CHILDREN :

1   Edna⁸ Woods, b. April 11, 1877.
2   Robert⁸ Woods, b. May 7, 1879.
3   William⁸ Stansbury, b. Oct. 25, 1880.
4   John⁸ Blair, b. Sept. 21, 1882.
5   Donald⁸, b. Aug. 17, 1884.
6   Clinton⁸ Irving, b. Aug. 21, 1889.

JOSEPH⁴ (Zebulon³, Daniel², William¹)

Noted by Stryker ("Officers and Men of New Jersey," page 471) as sergeant of militia.   There is record of his serving during Washington's retreat through New Jersey in 1776, at the battle of Monmouth, at Springfield, at Connecticut Farms, and when the Pennsylvania line revolted in 1781.   He lived in Mendham Township, Morris County, N. J., near Basking Ridge in Somerset. His farm is still in possession of his descendants. He married, April 14, 1778, Martha Pierson.   He died November 8, 1822.

CHILDREN :

1   Uriah⁵, b. March 27, 1779.
2   Shadrach⁵, b. March 25, 1781.
3   Rebecca⁵, b. June 2, 1783.

4   Jonathan⁵, b. Feb 18, 1787.
5   Elizabeth⁵, b. June 19, 1789.
6   Martha⁵ S., b. Sept. 27, 1792.
7   James⁵, b. July 4, 1796.
8   Joseph⁵ P., b. Nov. 9, 1798.

JOSEPH⁵ PIERSON (Joseph⁴, Zebulon³, Daniel², William¹)

Lived at the old homestead in Mendham Township. Married, November 13, 1821, Persis Horton.

CHILDREN :

1   Nancy⁶ C., b. Aug. 21, 1824; m. Stephen D. Axtelle, and lives in Minneapolis, Minn.
2   Sarah⁶ Stewart, b. Oct. 14, 1827.
3   Caroline⁶ Wells, b. March 4, 1832; m. Babbitt.
4   Daniel⁶ Stewart, b. Jan. 19, 1835.
5   Henry⁶ Horton, b. Feb. 15, 1838.   (Lives at the old homestead.)
6   John⁶ Stewart, b. Sept. 12, 1841.
7   Charles⁶ Albert, b. June 17, 1843.

AUTHORITIES.

1. Piscataway Records of Birth, Marriage, and Death, Transcribed by W. A. Whitehead, the historian, and now in the archives of the N. J. Historical Society at Newark.

2. Piscataway Town Book, at Piscataway.

3. Proprietary Records, Perth Amboy.

4. Savage's Genealogical Dictionary of New England.

5. Elizabethtown Bill in Chancery.

6. Vital Records of Rehoboth. James N. Arnold.

7. MS. Copy of Woodbridge Records. New York Genealogical Society.

8. Woodbridge and Vicinity. Rev. Joseph Dally.

9. Records of the Estate of James Alexander of New Jersey, in the archives of the N. J. Historical Society.

10. Trustee Book of Basking Ridge Presbyterian Church.

11. Winsor's History of Duxbury, Mass.

12. Dean's History of Scituate, Mass.

13. Contributions to East Jersey History. W. A. Whitehead.

14. History of Middlesex County, N. J. Woodford Clayton.

15. Records of First Baptist Church at Morristown, N. J.

16. MSS., Family Records, and Pedigrees in private hands.

17. Records in Pension Office at Washington.

18. Doty Genealogy.

19. Records in State Library at Trenton, N. J.

20. Passaic Valley Genealogies. John Littell.

21. Early Germans of New Jersey. Rev. T. F. Chambers.

22. Gravestones at Piscataway.

ADDENDA.

The following family belongs probably among the descendants of John² Sutton, as the similarity of locality and of names suggests. See family of John³ Sutton (John², William¹), and note. Probably 4th generation.

E.F.H.S.

REV. ABNER⁴ SUTTON

Born May 8, 1741, near Basking Ridge, in Bernard Township, Somerset County, N. J. He married, May 31, 1768, Mary Davison, born May 12, 1742. He died February 26, 1795. He was a Baptist minister.

CHILDREN :

1 Sarah⁵, b. April 11, 1769; d. Nov. 30, 1812.
2 A son⁵, b. Dec. 25, 1770; d. Jan. 27, 1771.
3 David⁵, b. about 1771; d. May 14, 1852.
4 George⁵, b. Jan. 8, 1773; d. ———.
5 Jeremiah⁵, b. Aug. 8, 1774; d. May 8, 1848.
6 John⁵, b. Feb. 25, 1776; d. May 15, 1779.
7 Rozanna⁵, b. Nov. 15, 1780; d. April 28, 1811.
8 John⁵, b. Sept. 3, 1783; d. Oct. 31, 1806.

GEORGE⁵ (Abner⁴, ———³, John², William¹)

Married, November 23, 1805, Rebecca Conklin.

CHILDREN :

1 David⁶ Conklin, b. Aug. 27, 1806.
2 Ann Maria⁶, b. April 17, 1808.
3 Eliza⁶, b. Feb. 1, 1810.
4 John⁶ Conklin, b. Jan. 12, 1811.

ADDENDA

By the Author

Edward F. H. Sutton

No birth record of WILLIAM SUTTON
of Eastham has ever been found, but recent
researches (1934-35)-- and rather those of
Mr. William A. Whitcomb, of Boston, than
the writer's own -- have developed presumptive evidence that he was a son of GEORGE
SUTTON of Scituate. On the other hand
there is nothing at all to indicate that
WILLIAM could have been a son of JOHN SUTTON
of Hingham, regarding whom the facts are as
follows:

I.   JOHN SUTTON of Attleborough in
Norfolk came in the ship Diligent in 1638
with a wife and four children, and settled
at Hingham, Massachusetts Colony.   His
wife's name was JULIEN, or JULIENNE; since
he is called "Senior", one of the children
was certainly a son JOHN, and it is a fair
inference that the following were his daughters.

HANNAH, died in Hingham, October, 1642.
ESTHER, married in Rehoboth 1646.
ANNE,   married in Rehoboth 1651.
MARGARET, married in Rehoboth 1655, and

presumably born in New England, since there
were but four children in the immigrant
party.

JOHN SUTTON, SENIOR, removed 1643-1644 to the distant inland town of Rehoboth, where he spent the rest of his life and died June 1, 1670. His wife JULIANNA was buried at Rehoboth June 4, 1678.

JOHN (2) SUTTON, the only discoverable son of JOHN (1) apparently first resided at Hingham. He removed to Scituate in Plymouth Colony and while resident there on December 2, 1653 sold the lands "which the town of Hingham gave to JOHN SUTTON, my father." He is repeatedly mentioned in the Scituate records, married there Elizabeth House, had a numerous family and died there 1691; his will of date November 12 stating him to be "aged 70 or thereabouts." This dates his birth 1620-21, necessarily in England, and fixes his identity as the son of JOHN (1) (Mayflower Descendant. Vol. 31, 1933). Yet this is the man whom Deane's History of Scituate and Savage's Genealogical Dictionary (copying Deane) call son of GEORGE SUTTON! This is not the only error that Deane makes about the Sutton line as is shown by comparison with the Mayflower Descendant. Vols. 10 and 13.

JOHN (2) SUTTON of the Hingham line, is ancestor of all the SUTTONS of Scituate. The name survived in the town until the second quarter of the 19th century. GEORGE SUTTON of Scituate, on the other hand, left no descendants there, as will presently be shown.

II.   GEORGE SUTTON sailed 1634 on
the ship Hercules of Sandwich, Kent, as a
servant in the party of Nathaniel Tilden,
of Tenterden, in the same county.   The
poorer Puritans often worked their passage
in this way with wealthier relatives or
friends; at all events, within two years of
the party's establishment at Scituate
GEORGE married Nathaniel's daughter, Sarah
Tilden.   Nathaniel Tilden, it may be mentioned, though a merchant, was of aristocratic
connections, and descended of a very ancient
Kentish family.   His departure for New
England was thought worthy of note in
a History of Sandwich published in 1792.
A pedigree compiled in Elizabethan times
by the famous antiquary, Camden, is still
in possession of English representatives
of the name, tracing their descent from
Sir William Tylden de Sittenbourne and
Congleton, Cheshire, "who fought in ye Van
of ye English Armie commanded by Lord Audley
under ye Black Prince at ye Battle of
Poictiers Anno 1356."   In New England
Nathaniel Tilden, styled "Gentleman",
was at once accorded the position due to
his social status, education and comparative
wealth.   He was an elder of the church
and held important offices of trust.

On this same voyage of the Hercules
in 1634 came SIMON SUTTON as a servant in
the party of William (1) Hatch.   He is
evidently nearly akin to GEORGE SUTTON, but
his name disappears from the records, and

beyond the fact that he served as a witness
to the will of Nathaniel Tilden in 1641,
nothing is known of him. William (1) Hatch
had a son William (2) Hatch, also a passenger
on the Hercules, and the intimate nature of
the friendship between the latter and GEORGE
SUTTON is of particular interest. William
died in Virginia in 1657. Before he undertook that long and dangerous journey he made
his will, and entrusted the keeping of it --
not to his own brother-in-law, Lieutenant
James Torry, the Town Clerk, but to GEORGE
SUTTON (Mayflower Descendant.)

Nathaniel Tilden died in 1641, and
the following year his widow Lydia married
Timothy Hatherley, who thus became step-
father-in-law of GEORGE SUTTON. Hatherley
and his lifelong friend, James Cudworth, men
of the very first prominence in Plymouth
Colony, were liberals in principle. When
Plymouth, following the lead of Massachusetts,
enacted penal laws against the Quakers, these
two alone, of all the magistrates, entered
a strong protest. They paid for their
temerity by the loss of political position
and influence. Cudworth was, indeed, fined
for holding intercourse with Quakers (merely
with the intention of discovering their
tenets) and eventually disfranchised, but he
lived to see the turn of the tide and to be re-
seated as a magistrate. Hatherley died while
still under the ban.

Their courage bore fruit. Their
personal influence was such that the Plymouth penal laws, though similar to those
of Massachusetts were not enforced with
the Massachusetts rigor. No Quaker suffered death in Plymouth, and Quaker congre-
gations, barely tolerated at first, sprang
up and eventually flourished, particularly
on Cape Cod.

As might have been expected, one
such developed at Scituate, the home town
of Hatherley and Cudworth, which eventually
attracted members of some of the best of the
local families, including Cudworth's own.
But it grew slowly and was not numerous
enough to need a meeting house until 1676.
Ten years before that date, or about the
year 1668, GEORGE SUTTON, who had been so
intimately associated with the disinterested
champions of Quakerism, emigrated with most of
his family to North Carolina.

Anglican Virginia had not been so hard
on the Quakers as Puritan New England. George
Fox found them numerous there when he visited
the Old Dominion in 1672. The northern parts
of North Carolina, when opened for settlement
a few years earlier, received Quakers along
with other Virginia immigrants; indeed Bancroft
exaggerates so far as to say that North Carolina
was settled by Quakers! While that is not the
case, it is certain that the complete religious
freedom of a new and unorganized province was

attractive to many settlers, and certain
it is that after Fox's missionary visit of
1672, the sect grew and flourished amazingly
in North Carolina, so that before the end
of the century a Quaker had been elected
Governor.   In no other Colonial Province
excepting Pennsylvania and West Jersey,
were the Quakers so numerous and powerful.

It is fair to conclude that Quaker
faith had as much to do with GEORGE SUTTON'S
removal to North Carolina as with WILLIAM
SUTTON'S to Piscataway.   That GEORGE and
his family were Quakers in their new home,
there is small doubt.   One of the earliest
Quaker meeting houses in the Province was
built towards the end of the 17th century on
"Sutton's Creek" so called because it marched
with the lands of GEORGE or his sons.   JOSEPH,
one of the latter, married Deliverance
Nicholson, whose family had suffered per-
secution for Quakerism in New England.   GEORGE
settled in that part of the Province that,
after bearing various other names, is now
Perquimans County and left a numerous posterity.
He died there April 12, 1669 aged about 56.
His wife Sarah Tilden died there March 20, 1677
aged 64.   She was born at Tenterden in Kent,
1613, and baptized there in St. Mildred's
Church, January 13.   The two compilers of
this record arrange their family as follows,
adding on presumptive evidence, the sons
DANIEL and WILLIAM.

Children of GEORGE SUTTON and SARAH
TILDEN, all born in Scituate, Plymouth Colony.

1. JOSEPH   b. about 1637
                    m. 168-, Deliverance Nicholson.
                    d. 1695 Perquimans Co.

2. DANIEL   b. about 1639
                    m. 1667 at Charlestown, Mass.
                    Mary Cole. (Probably daughter
                    of Isaac Cole of Charlestown,
                    a passenger on the Hercules
                    with GEORGE SUTTON and the
                    Tildens.) He had in Charles-
                    town a son, DANIEL.
                    d. 1711, Burlington, N. J.

3. WILLIAM   b. about 1641.
                    m. 1666 Damaris Bishop.
                    d. about 1713, Piscataway, N. J.

4. NATHANIEL b. about 1643.
                    m. 1668 in Virginia, Deborah Astine.
                    d. 1682, Perquimans Co.

5. LYDIA   Baptized September 13, 1646.

6. SARAH   "   December 3, 1648. Died
                            in infancy.

7. SARAH   "   September 15, 1650.
                          m. Perquimans Co. 1668
                          John Barrow.

8. ELIZABETH "   August 28, 1653, m. Per-
                          quimans Co. 1674 Ralph
                          Fletcher. d. 1700.

GEORGE SUTTON of Scituate, married 1636, (March 13) has no child recorded in the New England archives until 1646, and then a succession of daughters. The compilers of this record undertook to fill in this ten year gap, and succeeded in finding in the North Carolina archives, the sons NATHANIEL and JOSEPH.

Now as to WILLIAM and DANIEL.

WILLIAM first appears in 1666 on Cape Cod at Barnstable, a town which was founded 1639-1640 by a mass emigration from Scituate led by the Rev. John Lothrop. The early relations between the two towns were, therefore, particularly close. The earliest church records of Scituate are still preserved at Barnstable, whither they were carried when the latter was founded.

For the love of laughter, it should be noted that WILLIAM makes his first appearance in history because of his borrowing -- quite un-authorizedly -- the Bible from the Barnstable meeting house. When caught, he was not frank about the matter, and so, June 5, 1666, he was hailed to court, and fined for purloining the Bible "one pound, and for telling a lye about the same, ten shillings." His departure from the town was probably expedited by these oc-currences, and a few weeks later at the neighbor-ing settlement of Eastham, he took refuge in matrimony with Damaris Bishop.

WILLIAM SUTTON was a Quaker. If he was

a son of GEORGE of Soituate, as we believe,
one might suppose he was named for William
Hatoh, his father's most intimate friend.
Again one might suppose that the names of
his mother's family, the Tildens, would re-
appear in that of WILLIAM.   This is so far
the case that three of WILLIAM'S children,
THOMAS, MARY and JOSEPH, bear the names of
their Tilden uncles and aunt.   Lastly,
WILLIAM had a son DANIEL.   Now the DANIEL
whom we believe to have been son of GEORGE
of Soituate, and who first appears at
Charlestown, with wife MARY and son DANIEL
(Charlestown being a part of Boston, and
Soituate being located almost on Boston
Harbor) was a Quaker, and left descendants
at Burlington, in the Quaker colony of West
Jersey, some forty miles by the New York -
Philadelphia post road from Piscataway in
East Jersey, where WILLIAM resided.   In
1706 it is recorded that WILLIAM thought
of removing thence to Burlington.   DANIEL
is mentioned frequently in the Burlington ar-
chives and once in connection with a RICHARD
SUTTON, otherwise unrecorded, who may have
been the RICHARD who was WILLIAM'S son.

      Thus, times, places, religions, and
family names concur so well, that WILLIAM
and DANIEL have been tentatively interpolated
among the children of GEORGE and SARAH
SUTTON.

AUTHORITIES:

Mayflower Descendant.
Plymouth Colony Records.
Vital Records of Rehoboth.
Deane's History of Scituate.
Winslow's History of Perquimans County,
      North Carolina.
Archives of New Jersey, Abstracts of Wills, etc.
Tilden Genealogy.

Edward Forrester Holden Sutton

New York, N. Y. 1935

Lightning Source UK Ltd.
Milton Keynes UK
UKHW021950311022
411405UK00007B/1270